ENIGMAS *of* HISTORY

THE MYSTERIES OF
THE TROJAN WAR

WORLD
BOOK

a Scott Fetzer company
Chicago
www.worldbook.com

World Book edition of "Enigmas de la historia" by Editorial Sol 90.

Enigmas de la historia
La guerra de Troya

This edition licensed from Editorial Sol 90 S.L.
Copyright 2013 Editorial Sol S.L. All rights reserved.

English-language revised edition copyright 2014
World Book, Inc.
Enigmas of History
The Mysteries of the Trojan War

World Book, Inc.
233 North Michigan Avenue
Suite 2000
Chicago, Illinois, 60601 U.S.A.

For information about other World Book publications,
visit our website at **www.worldbook.com** or call
1-800-967-5325.

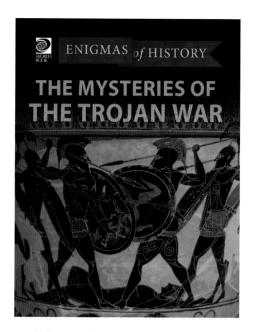

Detail of a piece of black-figure pottery from ancient
Greece, dating to around 530 B.C. The image on this
calyx-krater (wine bowl) depicts a battle scene from
Homer's *Iliad.*

© Prisma Archivo/Alamy Images

Library of Congress Cataloging-in-Publication Data

Guerra de Troya. English.
  The mysteries of the Trojan War. -- English-language revised edition.
    pages cm. -- (Enigmas of history)
  Summary: "An exploration of the questions and mysteries that have
puzzled scholars and experts about the Trojan War. Features include a
map, fact boxes, biographies of famous experts on the archaeology of
the area in which the war is thought to have taken place, places to see
and visit, a glossary, further readings, and index"-- Provided by
publisher.
  Includes index.
  ISBN 978-0-7166-2668-8
  1. Trojan War--Juvenile literature. 2. Turkey--Antiquities--Juvenile
literature. 3. Troy (Extinct city)--Juvenile literature. I. World Book, Inc.
II. Title.
DF221.T8M96 2014
939'.21--dc23
                                                    2014007070

Set ISBN: 978-0-7166-2660-2

Printed in China by PrintWORKS Global Services,
Shenzhen, Guangdong
1st printing May 2014

Staff

Contents

The Trojan War

Myth (a legend or story of unknown origin) delights the public, but it makes scholars nervous. Scholars accept the archaeologists' reconstruction of the history of the Bronze Age—that is, of Greece and the Near East from around 3,100 to 1,200 B.C.—from material culture and written evidence dug from the earth. Yet often the claims of literature are not seen as a view into history.

The Trojan War is an example of this attitude. It is one of the most famous events of the ancient world, but scholars have long doubted whether it even happened. In ancient times, even the most hard-headed of the Greeks and Romans accepted the war as historical fact. Modern scholars, however, are more skeptical. After all, the most famous text about the war, the *Iliad* by Homer, is an *epic poem* (a long narrative poem), not a history book. It contains many supernatural events, and it was written centuries after the supposed war it describes. The Trojan War, if it took place, probably occurred around 1200 B.C., while the *Iliad* and *Odyssey* probably date to around the 700's B.C.

Yet, ever since 1871, when Heinrich Schliemann began excavating a mound in northwest Turkey near the entrance to the Dardanelles (a strait that joins the Aegean Sea with the Sea of Marmara), the evidence has mounted that Troy was real and the Trojan War was based on a kernel of historical events. Schliemann claimed to have found the ruins of Troy. He was an amateur, but in the 140 some years since, professional archaeologists have re-excavated the site in a scientific manner. Meanwhile, excavations in Greece have found a great Bronze Age civilization there as well—the Mycenaean (MY suh NEE uhn) culture—whose sites would have made worthy homes for the likes of the Greek warrior Achilles and Agamemnon, king of the southern Greek city of Mycenae.

New excavations at Troy since 1988 have led to dramatic discoveries. Although previously Troy looked small, poor, and perhaps only a fortress, we know now that Troy was a big, rich city. Although earlier excavators suspected the inhabitants of Troy were actually Greeks, new evidence shows that they were Anatolians (from a region located in the Asian part of modern Turkey). They probably spoke a language closely related to that of the great kingdom that dominated Anatolia, the Hittites—another great civilization uncovered by archaeology.

A few scholars have criticized the methods of the post-1988 excavations at Troy, but it is difficult to discount the evidence of Hittite-language inscriptions. They show continual attacks on Anatolia's coast mounted from the sea by the Greeks. They reveal a kingdom known variously as Taruisa and Wilusa—the city that Homer calls Troy and Ilion, if you will—squeezed between Greeks and Hittites.

Meanwhile, Linear B, the script used to write early Greek, shows that a large percentage of the names in Homer's writings are found during the Bronze Age, but not later. The *Iliad* includes a highly accurate list of Greek cities as they were 500 years earlier. Texts from far afield—from Egypt, Canaan, Syria, and Mesopotamia—show that deeds in Homer that once seemed unlikely sometimes actually reflect Bronze Age customs of the ancient Near East.

It even seems possible that the Greeks went to war over a stolen princess. Not that Helen is a historical figure; we can't be sure if she existed. But we do know that Bronze-Age kings fought battles over family quarrels and personal insults.

In short, we know that a vibrant, exciting, and historical world surrounds the tales of Homer's heroes. Even the greatest products of the human imagination may sometimes be grounded in fact.

The Story of the War

According to ancient Greek myths, the Trojan War resulted from an incident at the wedding feast of Peleus, the king of Phthia, and Thetis, a sea goddess. All the gods and goddesses had been invited except Eris, the goddess of discord. Eris was offended, so she sent a golden apple inscribed "For the most beautiful." Three goddesses—Hera, Athena, and Aphrodite—each claimed the apple, and a quarrel began. Paris, the son of King Priam of Troy, judged the dispute. He awarded the apple to Aphrodite because she promised him Helen, the most beautiful woman in the world.

Helen was already married to King Menelaus of Sparta. But when Paris visited her, she fled with him to Troy. Menelaus and his brother, Agamemnon, organized a large Greek expedition against Troy to win Helen back. The Greek army included such heroes as Achilles, Ajax the Greater, Nestor, and Odysseus (*Ulysses* in Latin).

The Greek army laid siege to Troy for 10 years but could not conquer the city. Homer's *Iliad* describes some of the events that occurred during the last year of the struggle. The war began to go badly for the Greeks after Achilles, their greatest warrior, left the battlefield. Achilles refused to fight because Agamemnon, the Greek commander, had insulted him. The Trojans, led by Hector, drove the Greeks back to their ships. Achilles finally returned to combat after his best friend, Patroclus, had been slain by Hector. Achilles killed Hector to avenge Patroclus's death.

The *Iliad* ends with Hector's funeral, and Greek legends relate the events that followed. The Trojans received help from their allies, the Ethiopians and an army of women warriors called Amazons. But Achilles helped the Greeks to defeat their enemies by killing Penthesilea, the queen of the Amazons, and Memnon, the king of the Ethiopians. Paris, aided by the god Apollo, later shot Achilles in the heel with an arrow and killed him.

The fall of Troy is described in the *Aeneid* (ih NEE ihd), a later work by the Roman poet Virgil. The Greeks built a huge wooden horse, which has become known as the Trojan horse, and placed it outside the walls of Troy. Odysseus and other warriors hid inside the horse while the rest of the Greek army sailed away.

The Trojan prophetess Cassandra and the priest Laocoon (lay OK oh on) warned the Trojans against taking the horse into their city. But Sinon, a Greek prisoner, persuaded the Trojans that the horse was sacred and would bring the protection of the gods. The Trojans pulled the horse into Troy. That night they fell asleep after celebrating their apparent victory. Odysseus and his companions then crept out of the horse and opened the city gates for the rest of their warriors, who had returned from a nearby island.

The Greeks took back Helen, killed almost all the Trojans, and burned Troy. According to the *Aeneid*, the few Trojan survivors included the warrior Aeneas (ih NEE uhs), whose descendants founded Rome.

A Bronze Age Epic

The Trojan War was described in a cycle of poems—the *Iliad* and the *Odyssey*. Both of these poems are credited to Homer, though whether there was an actual Greek poet named Homer is still debated by experts.

A Greek poet of around the time of the 700's B.C., whom we call Homer, gave wings to the epic ballads of oral tradition about the legendary Trojan War. The poet's work was eventually called "the first masterpiece of Western literature." While myths are not history, Troy became part of past events worth remembering, and people didn't know how to distinguish the line between fiction and reality. In the *hexameters* (poetry with lines made up of six feet, or measures) of the *Iliad,* an epic of 24 books, the human and the divine merge, riding through war and death and from rage to mercy. The legends of this world, populated by gods and heroes, traveled and grew by word of mouth thanks to the *aoidos* (bards), in an era when writing was not yet commonplace. Even-

tually it took the permanent form of the Homeric poems, both in the *Iliad* as well as in the *Odyssey* that followed. Homer's work was highly respected, memorized by intellectual youth at an early age, and passed down through generations.

The first song of the *Iliad* begins by telling of the 10th and last year of the Trojan war, in the middle of a plague sent by the god Apollo to the campsite of the *Achaeans* (people from a region of ancient Greece), invaders from the north. A sense of the formation of a Greek identity was developing during the era of the Mycenaean civilization (at its height from 1500 to 1200 B.C.). This Greek unity began in the Peloponnesus (PEHL uh puh NEE suhs), the southern peninsula of Greece. In time it extinguished the seafaring prominence of the 11 centuries of the Minoan civilization

(2600-1500 B.C.), which had flourished on the island of Crete.

At the start of the *Iliad,* the future loomed dark for the Achaean military expedition, whose intent was to punish the Trojans for stealing Helen, wife of Menelaus, king of Sparta. Her theft by Priam's son Paris began an earthly conflict that mobilized both the immortal gods and earthly heroes.

SETTING OF THE WAR

The poetic setting of the war is in Asia Minor, near the western entrance of the Hellespont, now called the Strait of the Dardanelles, which connects the Aegean Sea with the Marmara and the Black Seas (see map on pages 16-17). The Homeric poems narrate a story that is supposedly very ancient, but they also describe the setting of the society in which the author lived, in the 700's B.C.—toward the end of the

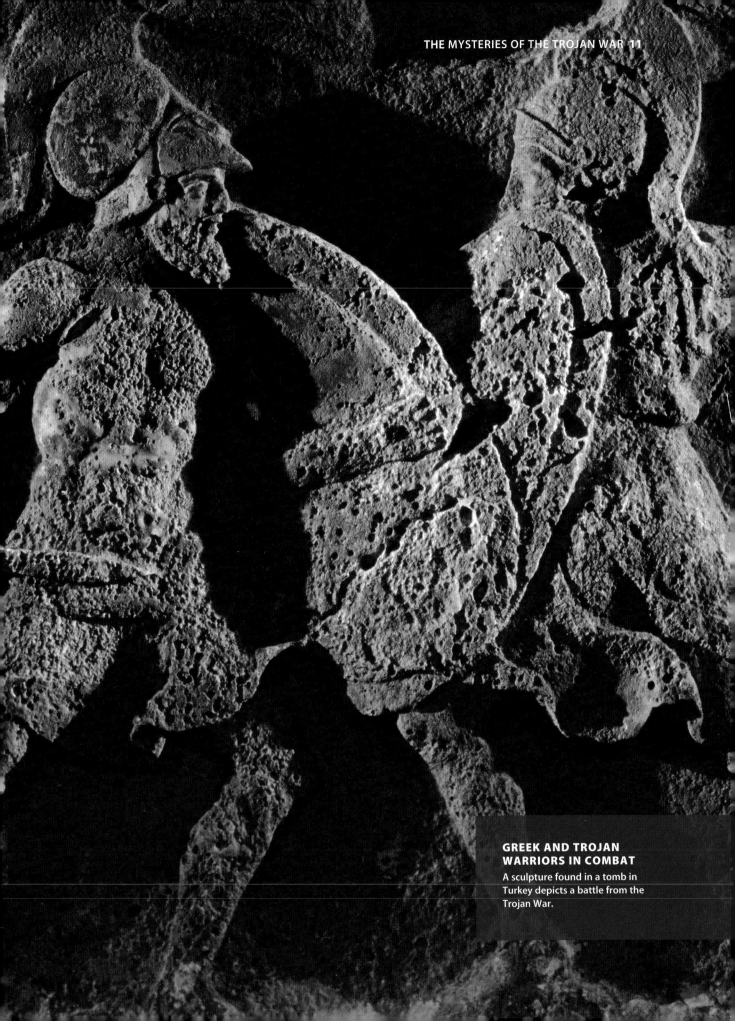

GREEK AND TROJAN WARRIORS IN COMBAT
A sculpture found in a tomb in Turkey depicts a battle from the Trojan War.

Dark Age of Greece and into the dawning of the *Archaic Period* (around 800 to 400 B.C. in ancient Greece). One thousand ships sailed from the port of Aulis in Boeotia (bee OH shuh), a district of ancient Greece that lay northwest of Athens, toward Troy. The ships were under the command of Menelaus's brother Agamemnon, king of Mycenae. Mycenae was a city-state of such importance that a whole era and civilization came to be identified as "Mycenaean." The fleet came together from various regions of Greece—Arcadia, Argos, Athens, Crete, Lacedaemonia, Myrmidon, and Salamina—and united to avenge the kidnapping of Helen. Ahead lay the Trojan army and their allies—the Dardanians and Phrygians of Anatolia and the Greek Pelasgians and Thracians. The gods were weaving the threads of the tragedy, deceiving the humans, making alliances and taking sides, handing out death on Earth as well as dissension on Mount Olympus.

The first book of the *Iliad* begins with Achilles, the son of Peleus, blaming Agamemnon for the plague because he did not return the prisoner Chryseis to her father Chryses, priest of Apollo. Agamemnon agrees to deliver her, but decides to take Briseis, Achilles's slave, for himself. This causes Achilles to retire from the war. At the request of the nymph Thetis, mother of Achilles, Zeus decides to favor Troy in battle. A duel is fought between Menelaus and Paris that ends with the intervention of Aphrodite—goddess of love and beauty. Then a battle takes place in which the Achaeans lose.

THE REASONS FOR THE WAR

The gods of Olympus were involved in the war from the start. Zeus himself intervened by summoning the attractive mortal Paris to help resolve the divine dilemma created by the golden apple (see page 8). Aphrodite was given the title of "the fairest" and in exchange granted Paris the love of Helen of Sparta, a woman of great beauty. The die was cast. It was not long before the Trojan War broke out in full force.

From the heights of Mount Ida, from the north face of which flowed the rivers of the Scamander and Simoeis, which ran alongside the city of Troy, Zeus enjoyed an excellent lookout point from which to follow the combat that took place on the Trojan plain. From the summit, known as the Gargarus, Zeus directed the course of the war in Olympic fashion. Then, Zeus fell into the trap his wife Hera had set and fell into a deep sleep. Poseidon, Zeus's brother, took advantage of this and helped the forces of Agamemnon. The awakening of Zeus settled things back into place. With defeat in sight, Achilles allowed his faithful friend Patroclus, leading troops of Myrmidons (MUR muh donz)—a people from Thessaly over whom Achilles was king), to help the Achaeans. Patroclus's attack against the walls of Troy, which were defended by the god Apollo, provoked Apollo's anger and incited Hector, brother of Paris, to join the combat. The *Iliad* draws to an end with the death of Patroclus at the hand of Hector, which unleashes a new outburst of rage from Achilles. After Achilles recovers the captive Briseis and reconciles with Agamemnon, he decides to return to the fight, wearing new weapons fabricated by the god Hephaestus (hih FEHS tuhs).

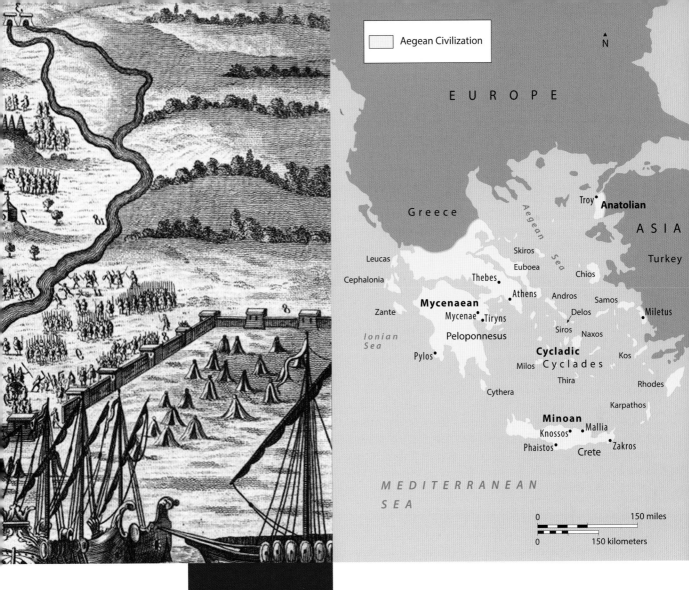

EUROPE

Greece

Leucas

Cephalonia

Zante

Ionian
Sea

Pylos

Thebes

Athens

Mycenaean

Mycenae · Tiryns

Peloponnesus

Cythera

Minoan

Knossos · Mallia

Phaistos · Zakros

Crete

Troy · Anatolian

ASIA

Turkey

Aegean Sea

Skiros

Euboea

Chios

Andros

Samos

Delos

Miletus

Siros

Naxos

Cycladic

Cyclades

Milos

Kos

Thira

Rhodes

Karpathos

MEDITERRANEAN
SEA

0   150 miles

0   150 kilometers

MAP OF TROY

Historical Troy was inhabited from around 3,000 B.C. It is located in present-day Turkey.

MAP OF CIVILIZATION ON THE AEGEAN SEA

The regions, cities, and sites of Aegean civilization, which existed on the islands and shores of the Aegean Sea between 3000 and 1100 B.C.

The goddess Athena, by order of Zeus, aids Achilles with ambrosia and nectar (food and drink of the gods). But Achilles's own horse, Xanthus, prophesies that his days are numbered. Each god and goddess supports his or her favorite hero for the coming battle. Achilles and Hector gain the spotlight, urging their troops into military action on the eve of a unique battle at the stone walls of Troy, where Achilles kills Hector. In the final song, the tragic-heroic vein of Homer continues, ending in a gesture of mercy. We first see Achilles, who is caught up in rage due to the funeral of his friend Patroclus, insult-ing the lifeless body of Hector. Achilles tied Hector's body behind his chariot and dragged it around the walls of Troy for several days. But, we then see a more merciful Achilles; he heeds the plea of the Trojan King Priam and returns to him the body of his son. And thus the *Iliad* comes to its end: In the house of Priam, with the funeral of Hector, the "tamer of horses."

Homer's following work, the *Odyssey*, is more optimistic. It is also made up of 24 books, this time with a happy ending. It describes the adventures of Odysseus on his dangerous return journey to his homeland, Ithaca (an island off the coast of Greece), after his victory in the Trojan War.

Some stories in the *Odyssey* flash back to the *Iliad*, such as the tale of the famous Trojan horse and the death of Achilles, which once again border on legend. In the eighth book of the *Odyssey*, the bard (singer-poet) Demodocus gives his account of the wooden horse filled with heavily armed warriors, which the Trojans hauled into the center of the city. The presumed gift from Odysseus brought great damage and death, including looting and fire. Meanwhile, the funeral of Achilles on the Trojan plain is told by Agamemnon at the beginning of the last book. It takes place on the plain of Asphodel (AS fuh dehl), a sort of "land of the dead." Achilles's horse predicted his death, but not its cause. As the legend goes, Paris fired an arrow that was guided by the god Apollo to the heel of Achilles—his only weak point. Apollo knew that, soon after Achilles was born, his mother, Thetis, had dipped him in the River Styx. The water of the Styx made Achilles immortal. However, the water did not touch the heel by which Thetis held him.

These events inspired seemingly endless legends: the kidnapping, the war, the horse, Homer the bard. These poetically connected events and personalities seemed to connect with reality on the day when German explorer Heinrich Schliemann (1822-1890), guided by the *Iliad*, began to head up an excavation team atop the mound of Hissarlik, located northwest of the Turkish peninsula of Anatolia. The land where the team worked was owned by the brother of Frank Calvert (1828-1908), a British government worker. Frank Calvert began digging at Hissarlik based on the thinking of the Scottish journalist Charles Maclaren (1782-1866). Maclaren was the first to think that Troy had been in the area of Hissarlik. Calvert himself had trusted his Trojan intuition to Schliemann, who got down to business in April 1870, digging until June 1873.

Schliemann, haunted by the Homeric poems since his childhood, set out to look for the lost city of Troy. After he became a millionaire, he divorced his Russian wife and wrote to the head of the Orthodox church in Athens with a request to find him a Greek woman who was versed in Homer. And so his 17-year-old Greek wife, Sophia, came on the expedition.

Schliemann took the verses of Homer to be the literal truth. Digging at Hissarlik, he discovered several overlapping layers of many other reconstructions of Troy. His excavation methods were unscientific. For lack of reliable studies of the archaeological layers, Schliemann assumed he had found Homeric Troy, and he collected precious objects for himself which he erroneously thought to be Priam's Treasure (see page 30).

In 1882, Schliemann collaborated with another German archaeologist, Wilhelm Dörpfeld (1853-1940), who categorized the various layers of the Hissarlik site, defining a total of nine. The top layer belonged to Roman Ilium, another name for Troy, from around 100 B.C., and the lowest one was built in approximately 3000 B.C. In 1890, Dörpfeld located the city of the *Iliad* at the level Troy VI, though his American colleague Carl W. Blegen (1887-1971), director of the excavations done by the University of Cincinnati between 1932 and 1938, thought it to be situated at Troy VII. Uncertainties remained regarding the history and the facts of the place.

For 50 years, the Trojan hill seemed to lose its attraction and excavation there was abandoned. Then, in 1988, a multinational and multidisciplinary team resumed the excavations under the direction of German Manfred Korfmann (1942-2005) of the University of Tübingen and American Charles Brian Rose of the University of Pennsylvania.

The *deciphering* (translating of code) of the small Hittite *cuneiform* (writing in wedge-shaped letters) tablets and other new archaeological findings reinforced the ideas on the existence of a Homeric Troy existing in the shadow of the neighboring Hittite kingdom. Troy's economic and military role in a region of high strategic value, as the only ocean port between the Aegean Sea and the Black Sea, was not to be underestimated. Likewise, Homer as a source cannot be discarded. The epic poems of the bard and their descriptions shed light on the history of this legendary city.

Manfred Korfmann
(1942-2005)

German archaeologist Manfred Korfmann's excavations in the 1990's continued the tradition of his German colleagues, in particular those of Schliemann. The studies and the digging he carried out south of the stone ruins already discovered at the top of Troy's *tell* (hill built up from layers of former sites) demonstrated that the dimensions of Troy were greater than those imagined until then.

Joachim Latacz
(1934-   )

Professor of classical *philology* (study of language) at the University of Basel, Latacz worked with Korfmann in excavations on the Trojan hill. He analyzed the *Iliad* to see if it was possible to establish a historical background for the poem.

Heinrich Schliemann

(1822-1890)

Inspired by the classical texts read to him by his father, Schliemann felt great admiration for the grand Homeric epics from an early age. After making a large fortune as a businessman, he decided to dedicate his time to archaeological research. In 1870, he discovered the ruins of Troy during an expedition to Hissarlik that he mostly financed himself, along with contributions by Frank Calvert, the British *consul* (an official appointed by a government to look after its commercial and cultural interests). The area that Schliemann excavated is known as "Troy VII." In order to get to it, Schliemann had to cut into the hill of Hissarlik. He used explosives that destroyed a good deal of the layers over Troy VII, thus ruining substantial archaeological information.

The scientific community objected strongly to his methods, but the studies of Schliemann—who later discovered a grave that he thought belonged to Agamemnon—undoubtedly helped to propel research regarding ancient Greece.

"I decided to devote myself to finding Troy the first time I heard a verse by Homer in Greek." H. S.

Carl Wiliam Blegen

(1887-1971)

Carl Blegen was an American archaeologist and professor at the University of Cincinnati, famous for his work on Pylos (in Greece) and Troy. His excavations in Troy were carried out between 1932 and 1938. One of the conclusions he drew was that the layer of Troy that corresponded to the city destroyed by the Achaeans and described by Homer was Troy VII-A. He dated the destruction of Troy around 1240 B.C. He also drew the conclusion that no one lived in Troy from 1240 until approximately 700 B.C., when it was colonized by the Greeks.

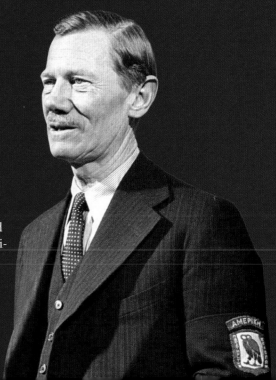

A Besieged City

The events of the long-besieged city of Troy are interwoven with Greek myths and legends. The confrontation between the Achaean armies and Troy is one of the central themes of the poems by Homer.

The Bronze Age in the Aegean

In the 1000's B.C., Troy had reached the height of its power and influence. It maintained significant relations with the Aegean world.

THE START OF THE CONFLICT

A Trojan prince, Paris, was sent to conduct diplomatic talks with Sparta, but he fell in love with Helen, kidnapped her, and took her to Troy as his wife. All the kings and princes of Greece united to plunder Troy.

HOMER, 800 TO 700 B.C.

The authorship of the two greatest epic works of ancient Greece—the *Iliad* and the *Odyssey*—are credited to Homer. His works describe the events of the Trojan War, including the kidnapping of Helen by Paris and the battle between Hector and Achilles.

① Agamemnon
King of Mycenae

Son of King Atreus of Mycenae and Queen Aerope, brother of Menelaus. When Agamemnon assumed his reign, he became the most powerful monarch in Greece. The *Iliad* mentions his dominion of the Peloponnesus.

② Menelaus
King of Sparta

Menelaus became the King of Sparta after being wed to Helen, daughter of Tyndareus, King of Sparta. Helen was abducted by Paris. Menelaus went to his brother Agamemnon to unite the Achaean army and recover Helen.

Chronology

The siege of Troy by the Achaeans lasted 10 years, until the city was finally conquered. The war happened during a period of changes in the Aegean and the rise of Mycenae.

1730 BC	1550 BC	1479 BC
Troy VI	**New Kingdom of Egypt**	**Battle of Megiddo**
The city occupies a strategic position, with access to the Black Sea. Troy was rebuilt more than 10 times due to catastrophes and occupations. It was destroyed by an earthquake around 1300 B.C.	The Theban ruler Ahmose I achieves the unification of Upper and Lower Egypt. With his military campaigns against the Hyksos and Asia Minor, he creates a militia which endures until 1070 B.C.	Pharaoh Thutmose III initiates combat against the Canaanite coalition of the king of Kadesh, in the city of Megiddo. The Egyptian victory allows dominion over the region of Canaan. The empire expands.

Did Cassandra predict Troy's end?

According to Greek mythology, the priestess Cassandra prophesied the destruction of Troy and the death of Agamemnon. However, she was unable to prevent these tragedies. The god Apollo loved Cassandra, but she did not return his love. He cursed her with the gift that her prophesies would always be true, but none would believe her.

Pontus Euxinus
(Black Sea)

Propontis
(Sea of Marmara)

Samothrace

Strait of
Helesponto

Lemnos

❸ Troy

MYSIA

ANATOLIA

Lesbos

Aegean
Sea

LYDIA

Chios

Chios

IONIA

Icaria   Samos

Icaria

Miletus

CARIA

Halicarnassus

Expanded
Area

Rhodes

MEDITERRANEAN
SEA

Rhodes

Thera

Knossos

❸ Priam

King of Troy

Son of Laomedan, Priam took charge of the kingdom at a very young age. He expanded his power throughout the region and positioned Troy as the dominant kingdom of Asia. His numerous descendants include Hector, Paris, Helenus, Deiphobus, Troilus, and Cassandra.

THE AEGEAN WORLD

- ● *Polis, Aegean cities*
- ○ Major cities under the dominion of Mycenae
- ➡ Possible route of military forces toward the city of Troy
- — Current borders

1450 BC	1380 BC	1300 BC	1250 BC
Mycenaean Civilization	**Hittite Empire**	**Splendor of Assyria**	**Trojan War**
An earthquake on the island of Thera produces a tsunami (large wave) that destroys the Cretan fleet. The sudden fall of the Minoan culture gives way to the dominance of Mycenae in the Aegean Sea.	Of Indo-European origin, the Hittites settle in the region of Anatolia, in Asia Minor. They become a power similar to Babylon and Egypt. They incorporate the use of iron and improve military chariots.	From the capital Assur, in the Valley of the Tigris River, the Assyrian King Tukulti-Ninurta I invades Mesopotamia and conquers Babylon. He governs the region.	The city of Troy VII is besieged by Mycenae. Around 1200 B.C., the downfall of the Mycenaean kingdom begins. Then came the migration of the Ionians and Aeolians toward the Cyclades and the coasts of Asia Minor.

The Power of Mycenae

In the middle of the Bronze Age, Mycenae united the Greek armies, leading them to Anatolia, or Asia Minor—a peninsula of western Asia between the Black Sea and the Mediterranean Sea—to conquer Troy. According to Homer, the Achaean forces comprised a total of 1,184 boats and 70,000 men. More recent calculations estimate a total of 300 ships and 15,000 men.

Mycenae versus Troy

Traditionally, the cause for the war is considered to be the abduction of Helen of Sparta. Another factor is that the wealth the Mycenaeans found in the Straits of Hellespont may have incited their greed.

Numbers to the left of characters' names correspond with numbers on the map, which designate the region for which a man fought.

MYCENAE

The Mycenaean civilization never reached the status of an empire. Their fearsome warriors were, however, powerful protagonists in the Mediterranean.

CHARACTERS WHO FELL IN BATTLE

	Soldier	Killed By
1	Amphimachus	Hector
2	Achilles	Paris
3	Greater Ajax	Suicide
4	Lesser Ajax	Poseidon
5	Antilochus	Memnon
6	Arcesilaus	?
7	Ascalaphus	Deiphobus
8	Clonius	?
9	Diores	?
10	Schedius	Hector
11	Eurytion	Eurypylus
12	Machaon	Eurypylus
13	Medon	Aeneas
14	Peneleos	Eurypylus
15	Patroclus	Hector
16	Podarces	Penthesilea
17	Protesilaus	Hector
18	Thersander	Telephus
19	Thersites	Achilles
20	Tlepolemus	Sarpedon

SURVIVING CHARACTERS

	Soldier		Soldier
21	Agamemnon	31	Philoctetes
22	Agapenor	32	Idomeneus
23	Antiphus	33	Menelaus
24	Automedon	34	Neoptolemus
25	Cyanippus	35	Meriones
26	Diomedes	36	Nestor
27	Eumelus	37	Odysseus
28	Euryalus	38	Podalirius
29	Eurypylus	39	Polypoetes
30	Phidippus	40	Thoas

The End of the War

After 10 years of laying siege, Odysseus of Ithaca devised the construction of a giant horse to be offered as a gift to the Trojans.

THE TROJAN HORSE

Greek soldiers were hidden inside the wooden horse. Surprised by the gift, the Trojans proclaimed themselves victorious, opened the gates and brought the horse in. During the night, the Achaean warriors came out of their hiding place and massacred their enemies.

Did the Trojan War happen as Homer said it did?

The wartime accounts of the Greek poet are still being debated because of their importance in Western culture. Such experts as the language specialist Joachim Latacz (see page 14) argue that these clashes were massive rather than individual, and that Homer, rather than describing the battlefield of the Bronze Age, was portraying military tactics of his time, shortly before the year 700 B.C.

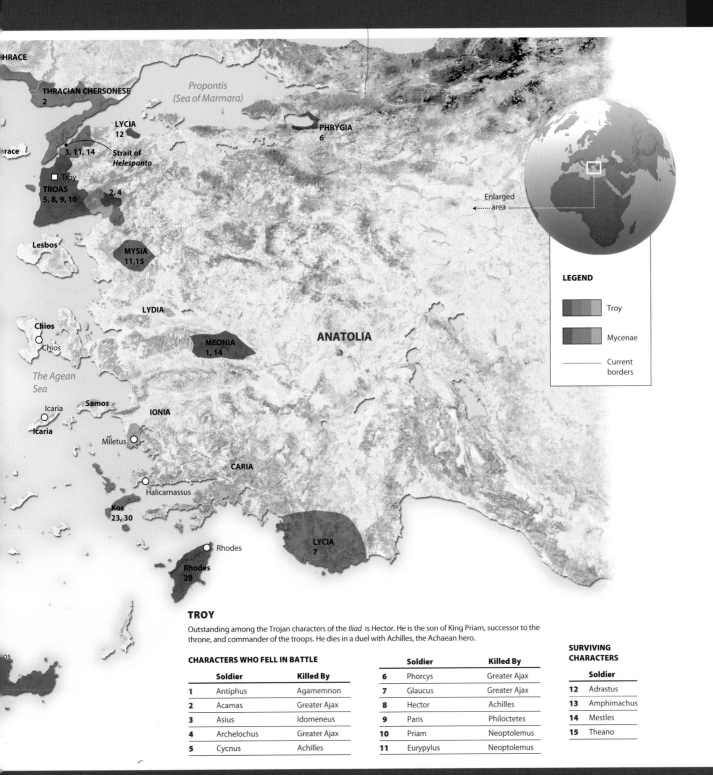

THRACE

THRACIAN CHERSONESE
2

Propontis
(Sea of Marmara)

LYCIA
12

PHRYGIA
6

3, 11, 14 — Strait of
Helesponto

Troy
TROAS
5, 8, 9, 10

2, 4

Lesbos

MYSIA
11, 15

LYDIA

MEONIA
1, 14

ANATOLIA

Chios
Chios

The Agean
Sea

Icaria
Icaria

Samos

IONIA

Miletus

CARIA

Halicarnassus

Kos
23, 30

Rhodes

LYCIA
7

Rhodes
20

Enlarged
area

LEGEND

	Troy
	Mycenae
	Current borders

TROY

Outstanding among the Trojan characters of the *Iliad* is Hector. He is the son of King Priam, successor to the throne, and commander of the troops. He dies in a duel with Achilles, the Achaean hero.

CHARACTERS WHO FELL IN BATTLE

	Soldier	Killed By
1	Antiphus	Agamemnon
2	Acamas	Greater Ajax
3	Asius	Idomeneus
4	Archelochus	Greater Ajax
5	Cycnus	Achilles

	Soldier	Killed By
6	Phorcys	Greater Ajax
7	Glaucus	Greater Ajax
8	Hector	Achilles
9	Paris	Philoctetes
10	Priam	Neoptolemus
11	Eurypylus	Neoptolemus

SURVIVING CHARACTERS

	Soldier
12	Adrastus
13	Amphimachus
14	Mestles
15	Theano

The Death of Patroclus

The death of Patroclus, friend to Achilles, the main Greek hero, is a turning point in the Trojan war. Achilles resolved to take revenge and carried it out by defeating and killing Hector, who had killed Patroclus in battle.

Achilles, the Avenger

When Achilles learned of the death of his friend, he ordered
the construction of a funeral pyre for him. He also cut off a lock
of his hair and made a sacrifice of oxen, lambs, dogs, horses,
and 12 noble youths from Troy. Afterwards, Achilles avenged
Patroclus's death by killing Hector.

Menelaus and Meriones recover the body of the fallen Patroclus from the battlefield,
depicted in a relief carved on an Etruscan urn from around the 100's B.C.

Did the War Really Happen?

Despite archaeological findings and the cuneiform tablets of the Hittites, which seem to provide plenty of evidence of the Trojan War, there are still researchers who question if it really happened.

The very name of Troy evokes the idea of war. The poems of Homer continue to fuel controversy between the power of the myth and the power of history. Could it be that imagination was the only possible way to explain the ancient world at that time?

In truth, the *Iliad* is an epic work that reflects with some precision a series of places, people, and traditions from the time of around 1300 B.C.

In the 1930's, U.S. archaeologist Carl Blegen observed the traces of a fire caused by an armed conflict in the layer that corresponds to Homeric Troy, the fire that may have led to its destruction. This layer was also found by the Korfmann-Rose team (see pages 14 and 25), which was formed around the Troy Project in 1988 and gave new energy to the excavation works at the mound of Hissarlik.

Before his death in 2005, Korfmann spread the word regarding the advances made by his team, which consisted of specialists of different disciplines and nationalities—mainly Germans, Americans, and Turks. Their research permitted the question of the existence of the Trojan War to be answered with a "yes." Korfmann also considered the possibility of more than one armed conflict at the same place around the end of the Bronze Age. It was clear that Troy had suffered several attacks and defended itself time and time again, as shown by the repairs made to the walls of the *citadel* (high, walled fortress) and the efforts to expand and strengthen them.

The discovery of a deep pit dug into the rock, forming the first obstacle for battle chariots, strengthened the theory of the defenders of the Homeric version.

NEW IDEAS

The new excavations revealed the remnants of a city complex dating to the same time period as

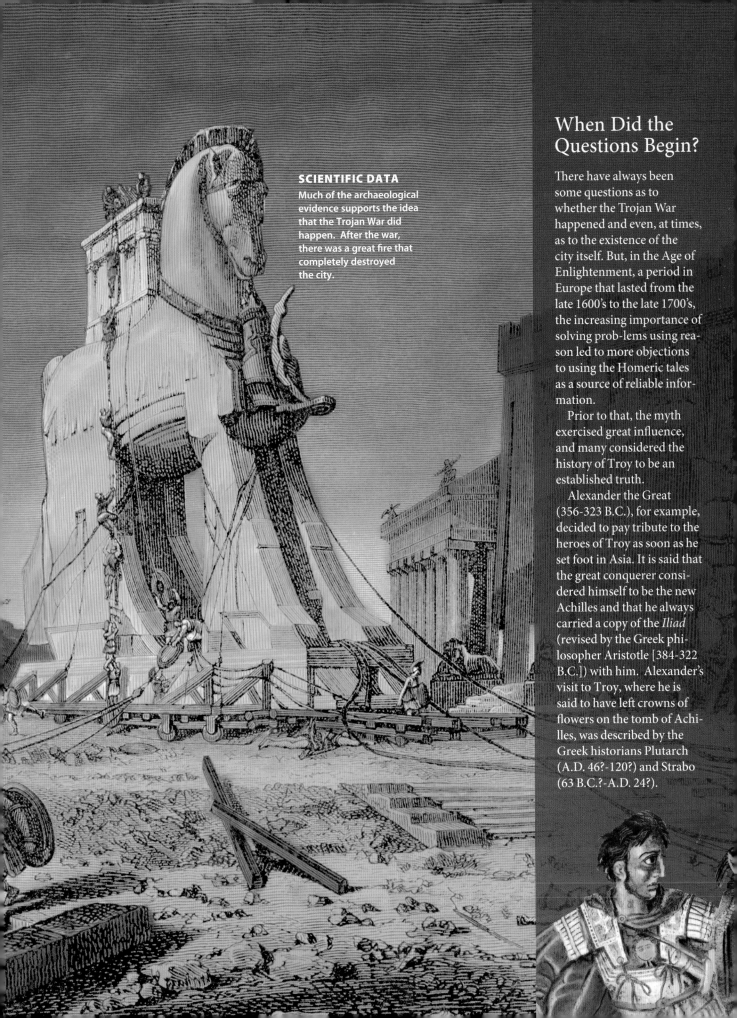

SCIENTIFIC DATA
Much of the archaeological
evidence supports the idea
that the Trojan War did
happen. After the war,
there was a great fire that
completely destroyed
the city.

When Did the Questions Begin?

There have always been some questions as to whether the Trojan War happened and even, at times, as to the existence of the city itself. But, in the Age of Enlightenment, a period in Europe that lasted from the late 1600's to the late 1700's, the increasing importance of solving prob-lems using rea-son led to more objections to using the Homeric tales as a source of reliable infor-mation.

Prior to that, the myth exercised great influence, and many considered the history of Troy to be an established truth.

Alexander the Great (356-323 B.C.), for example, decided to pay tribute to the heroes of Troy as soon as he set foot in Asia. It is said that the great conquerer consi-dered himself to be the new Achilles and that he always carried a copy of the *Iliad* (revised by the Greek phi-losopher Aristotle [384-322 B.C.]) with him. Alexander's visit to Troy, where he is said to have left crowns of flowers on the tomb of Achi-lles, was described by the Greek historians Plutarch (A.D. 46?-120?) and Strabo (63 B.C.?-A.D. 24?).

Opposing Views

Many scholars have held the same opinion as the well-known American-born British historian Moses Finley (1912-1986), who in his book *The World of Odysseus* questioned that the poems of Homer are historically true. Finley stated that "There is no presence of real Mycenaean elements in the Homeric poems, nor archaeological evidence that is actually valid which supports the historicity of the myth." His skeptical viewpoint opposes that held by several archaeologists convinced that the city exists, such as Heinrich Schliemann, Wilhelm Dörpfeld, Jerome Sperling, Carl Blegen, S. Hiller, and E. Demetriou. Finley always maintained that the *Iliad* was only put in writing around the end of the Greek Dark Age (1200-1100 B.C.) and that it says more about that period of history than about the Mycenaean period, even though things that no longer existed in the 700's B.C. are mentioned in the poem.

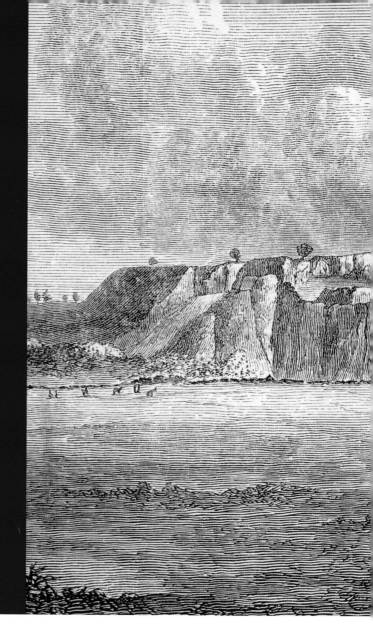

the Trojan War outside of the city walls, which came to be known as "the lower city." As a result, experts changed their ideas about the size and population of Troy, which was previously thought to have been limited to the area of the citadel. This expansion of the site, more consistent with the *Iliad*, also brought about the belief that it was a region of unquestionable geographic and political importance. Unlike Schliemann, Dörpfeld, and Blegen, who understood Troy to be a Greek settlement, the Korfmann-Rose team placed the Trojans in the zone of influence of Anatolia. A similar conclusion was reached after bringing together a large amount of evidence found at the archaeological site, from local ceramics and construction techniques to the remains from funeral rites.

The most valuable piece was discovered in 1995—a bronze seal with two names in Luwian hieroglyphs, an Anatolian language that is now extinct. The fact that the seal was in Luwian instead of Greek Linear B showed archaeologists that Trojans, and Troy, were in the sphere of Anatolia and the Hittite Empire, and not Greece.

Latacz, a well-known specialist on Troy and Homer, drew his ideas from both archaeological findings and the deciphering of Mycenaean, Hittite, and Egyptian clay tablets. Based on the Hittite text of the Alaksandu Treaty (from around 1280 B.C.), Latacz gained insight into the long and friendly relationship between the Trojans and the Hittites. This alliance was viewed negatively by the Achaeans, rivals of the Hittites in the region. Some cultures avoided direct confrontation and preferred to go to war against allies of their enemies. Troy, as part of the military "superpower" that was the Hittite empire, could have paid the price for a dangerous friendship.

THREAT AND TEMPTATION

Barry Strauss, Professor of History and Classics at Cornell University and expert in the military history of ancient Greece and Rome, never had doubts about the Trojan War. He trusted in the conclusions derived from stratigraphy, the

Key Information

The Trojan War occurred in the Bronze Age and was one of the last important events before the decline of the Mycenaean civilization. The principal enemy of the Mycenaeans was the Hittite Empire, which began in about 1650 B.C. Royal Hittite archives, written on clay tablets, have been preserved to this day and are a source of valuable information from that time period.

TELL OF HISSARLIK
It was designated as the possible site of Troy by several amateur archaeologists in the 1800's, including Frank Calvert and Heinrich Schliemann.

LUWIAN LANGUAGE
The Hittite texts are written in Luwian, which was spoken primarily in the southern and western areas of Anatolia.

The Troy Project

In the 1930's, an archaeological effort named the Troy Project began. It consisted of conducting excavations in the areas where the city from the Homeric tales supposedly existed. In 2009, the remnants of two humans and ceramic pieces that seem to be from 1200 B.C. were found. The team led in the 1990's by archaeologist C. Brian Rose (right), supported by William Aylward (left) and Cem Aslan (center) had some of the best results.

branch of geology that deals with the order and position of *strata* (layers of rock).

Troy simultaneously represented both a threat and a temptation for the Greeks (Achaeans or Mycenaeans at that time). It was a dagger aimed at the heart of Greece and a bridge to the center of the Hittite kingdom. It was also the most appealing and closest opportunity within reach for *plunder* (valuables carried off by invading soldiers during a war). It was also a crucial point in the region overall, including as a crossing point for goods from Syria, Egypt, occasionally the

Caucasus, and Scandinavia. However, it was clear to everyone that Troy would not be an easy city to conquer. Strauss described this perspective in the introduction to his book titled *The Trojan War: A New History* (2006). On the one side were the invaders, who lived miserably in tents and huts. And on the other side were the Trojans, who lived in luxury.

The Greeks, however, had at least three advantages: They were less civilized, more patient, and more mobile, mostly due to their ships. This was enough to help them triumph.

Underground Troy

Thanks to stratigraphic studies, 10 historical phases of the city made famous by the *Iliad* have been discovered. However, from the first settlement (2920-2450 B.C.) to Troy VII, as yet no written remains have been found. Such objects could greatly contribute to the historical and social understanding of Troy's development.

The War at level VIIa

From the discovery of type IIIb Mycenaean vessels (see below), it could be determined that the fire at Troy in level VIIa occurred between 1120 and 1180 B.C., a period that coincides with some of the dates estimated by classical authors for the end of the Trojan War, when the city would have been destroyed by the fire set by the Achaeans.

MYCENAEAN STYLE
Today, the time periods of Mycenaean ceramics and their differing styles are well known.

Stratigraphy at Troy

Stratigraphy involves the study and interpretation of layers of sedimentary rocks—those formed by the accumulation of sediment. The uppermost levels are those from the most recent time. Heinrich Schliemann knew that there were other layers of Troy between the burned-out layer likely from the Trojan War and the settlements from the Greco-Roman period. He just did not feel those layers were important. Professional archaeologists would disagree.

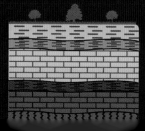

The Era of Large Walls

This drawing by Schliemann portrays the enormous walls of levels Troy III and IV, which he found during excavations in 1873. Built on the ruins of Troy II, Troy III (2350-2200 B.C.) was built almost completely from stone, unlike those versions before it, which were built from *adobe* (baked clay). *Anthropomorphic* vases (vases shaped like or in some way resembling humans) are characteristic of Troy III. Troy IV (2200-1900 B.C.) features the same wall technique as Troy II and Troy III, but the dome-shaped furnaces and dwellings with four rooms are new.

TROY IX, WELL-PRESERVED

This was the Roman city built by Gaius Flavius Fimbria, a man under the command of general Gaius Marius (157-86 B.C.), after the destruction of Troy VIII. Emperors Julius Caesar (100?-44 B.C.) and Augustus (63 B.C.-A.D.14) decorated it with temples and palaces. Ruins of this version of Troy are shown left.

Wilhelm Dörpfeld

This German archaeologist worked with Schliemann in Troy. In 1890, he found the remains of ceramics similar to those found in Mycenae. He reasoned that the layer of Troy VI dated to the same times as the peak of the Mycenaean civilization, and that layer could be identified with the city Homer wrote of in the *Iliad*.

The 10 Phases

After several excavations, a reconstruction was made of Troy's 10 phases of occupation. A long period of similar culture is observed from Troy I to Troy V.

Troy VI attests to a second expansion of the city, and Troy VII is clearly the main candidate for Homeric Troy.

BURIED MOAT

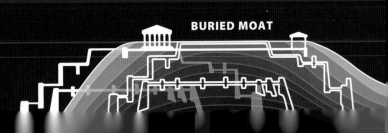

Was It Helen's Fault?

The role of Helen's beauty as the cause of the armed conflict between the Achaeans and the Trojans has been a subject of much debate. The legend of the beautiful woman has overshadowed the more likely reality of a trade war.

Helen of Troy has overshadowed Helen of Sparta. The theft of Helen has become the origin of the entire conflict, and her name is forever associated with the Trojan War. After the legendary event of Paris taking Helen from the house of her husband, Menelaus, in Sparta and bringing her to Troy, the message passed down through the ages has been of the destruction caused by a woman's beauty. Helen became "the face that launched a thousand ships": the most beautiful woman in the world, and the one who caused one of the most famous wars in history. Little has been mentioned about the destructive role of handsome, thoughtless Paris. He

is mostly considered to be in the background of two more important matters: the love of Helen and the death of Achilles. Helen of Sparta arrived in Troy by the will of the gods. Her name could well be seen as the poetic symbol of the Hellenic (Greek) nation. But perhaps the heart of the matter was hidden in the fiction of the *Iliad*. Was there a war caused by economic interests hidden behind the Homeric verses? In Homer's world, there was a great crisis in the second half of the 700's B.C., when the Hittites lost control of the copper mines east of Anatolia to the Assyrians (an ancient people who lived in a country in what is now modern-day northern Iraq). To improve the situation, the Hittites conquered Cyprus, rich in copper, and

established monetary penalties on trade in the eastern Mediterranean. This affected Achaean and Mycenaean ships. Homer's description of "Mycenae, rich in gold," really depicted Mycenae's prior glory. The Mycenaean civilization entered a period of decline as the result of the Hittite sanctions. Around the end of the 700's B.C., the Mycenaeans attempted a recovery, with acts of piracy and military expeditions to recover commercial navigation routes. One of its main objectives may have been Troy, the established gatekeeper from the Aegean Sea to the Black Sea. The Homeric statement "to fight for Helen and all of her wealth" may have been a justification hiding the primary cause of the conflict.

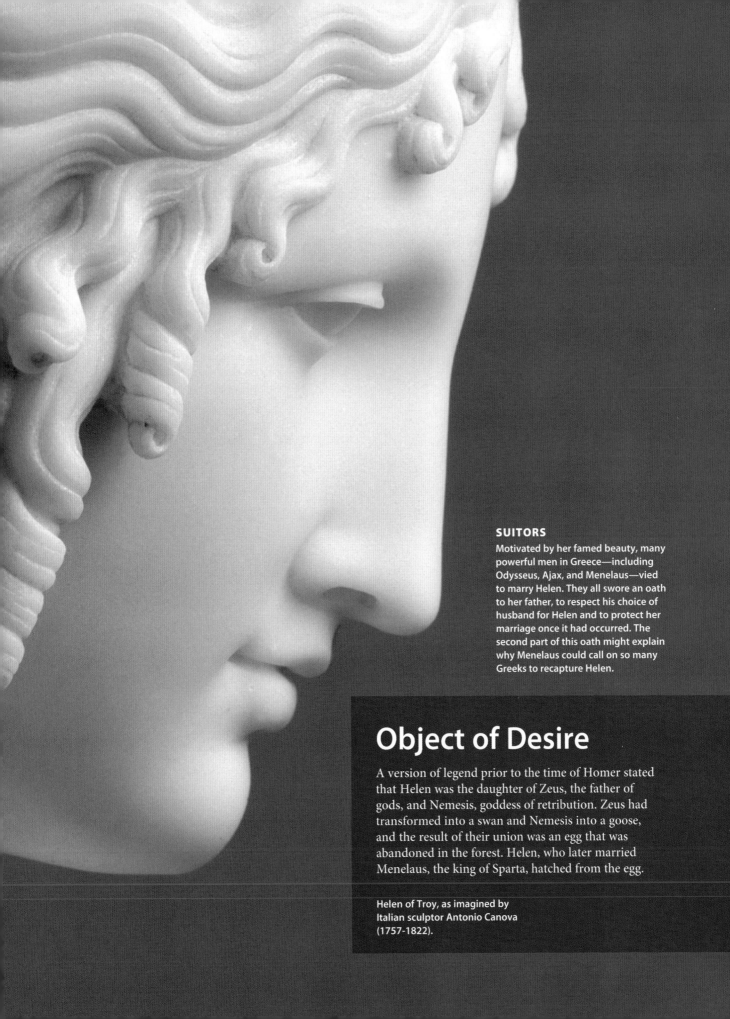

SUITORS

Motivated by her famed beauty, many powerful men in Greece—including Odysseus, Ajax, and Menelaus—vied to marry Helen. They all swore an oath to her father, to respect his choice of husband for Helen and to protect her marriage once it had occurred. The second part of this oath might explain why Menelaus could call on so many Greeks to recapture Helen.

Object of Desire

A version of legend prior to the time of Homer stated that Helen was the daughter of Zeus, the father of gods, and Nemesis, goddess of retribution. Zeus had transformed into a swan and Nemesis into a goose, and the result of their union was an egg that was abandoned in the forest. Helen, who later married Menelaus, the king of Sparta, hatched from the egg.

Helen of Troy, as imagined by Italian sculptor Antonio Canova (1757-1822).

Priam's Treasure

In 1873, during one of the many excavations carried out in the area of Troy, Heinrich Schliemann found a large quantity of objects of great archaeological value. He believed this treasure had belonged to the Trojan King Priam. Recent studies, however, date the objects to between 2670 and 2570 B.C., many hundreds of years before Homeric Troy.

Long Journey

Schliemann had the jewels from the treasure cache moved illegally to Greece. In 1874, he was accused by the Ottoman Empire of robbing national assets and sen-tenced to pay a fine. He paid a compensation and donated some of the treasure to the Museum of Constantinople so that the Turkish authorities would allow him to excavate in the future. After arriving in Berlin, the treasure was taken by the Red Army during the Second World War. Currently, it is loca-ted at the Pushkin Museum in Moscow.

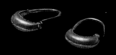

HIDDEN JEWELS
Before the Soviet Army took them, Schliemann's treasure was hidden in a specially built bunker beneath the Berlin Zoo.

DIADEMS
These diadems, or headpieces, were made out of gold with dangling ends in the shape of a leaf or flower. They were found inside golden jars that were among the treasure.

SOPHIA AS HELEN
Schliemann looked for a beautiful Greek woman interested in history and the poetry of Homer, and who was willing to travel. He found Sophia Engastromenos, the 17-year-old daughter of a textile trader; she fully assumed the role and became his wife. After the archaeologist found the jewels that supposedly belonged to Helen, Schliemann took the liberty of having Sophia try them on and pose for photos.

Frank Calvert, Pioneer

Hissarlik Hill, the place where Schliemann found Priam's Treasure (the illustration depicts the work in progress), had already been partially excavated by another amateur archaeologist, Frank Calvert, who went there because one of his brothers had bought land in the area. Around 1850, Calvert was already convinced of the presence of archaeological remains from Troy at the site.

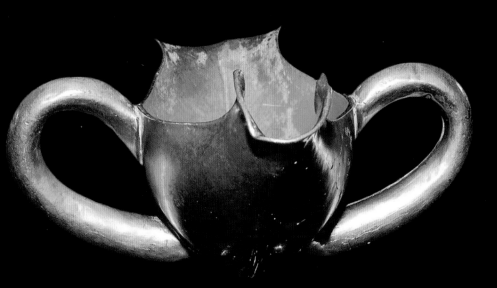

OUTSTANDING TREASURE

Among the objects found by Schliemann were copper cauldrons, gold and silver jars, 8,750 golden rings, and buttons and other small objects (necklaces and earrings). There were also six bracelets, two cups, and several bottles made of gold; some terracotta and electrum (an alloy of gold and silver) goblets, and six wrought silver knife blades.

AXES
Several small axes made out of ornamental stone.

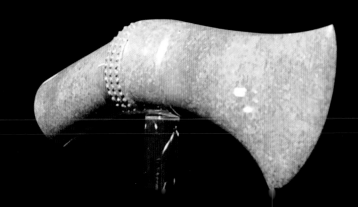

A Thousand Years Earlier

The large quantity of precious objects (more than 10,000 gold pieces) found by Schliemann had been hidden some 1,000 years before the events described by Homer in his epic poems. However,

Schliemann would never know this, because he would never find out that Homeric Troy was not Troy II, which he had excavated, but Troy VII, which he hardly touched in his early excavations.

Did a Poet Named Homer Exist?

All the information about Homer is based on guesses. Was his work written by only one author or a series of different authors?

It was the 700's B.C., and the Greek written alphabet had just been introduced, thanks to the Phoenicians. Now, a river of written legends could begin to flow, recording stories that until then had been circulating by word of mouth, from bard to bard, throughout the mysterious Dark Age of Greece.

Short poems were written and sung about the Trojan War during the 1100's B.C. onwards, in the palaces of the noble descendants of the Mycenaean kings. As for Homer, the presumed author of the *Iliad* and the *Odyssey*, it came to be said that he was a hostage, taking the Greek meaning of *homeros,* which meant *hostage* or *pledge,* literally. But no one went further than what resembled word play to actually figure out Homer's ancestry. According to tradition, Homer was born in Smyrna (a coastal city in modern-day Turkey), spent most of his life on the Greek island of Chios, and died on the Greek island of Ios. The only thing we know for certain is that Homer's work is the foundation upon which epic poems, and eventually Western literature, was built.

HERODOTUS'S BIOGRAPHY

One of the several biographies of Homer has been attributed to the "father of history," the Greek Herodotus, who lived between 484 and 424 B.C. In this record, Homer's name at birth was Melesigenes, son of the river-god Meles and the nymph Cretheis, who was related to the legendary Greek musician Orpheus and the Greek poet Hesiod. Homer is said to have adopted his famous name after he became blind. There is also a famous legend of the poetic conflict between Hesiod and Homer at the funerary games celebrated in Chalcis, a city on the island of Euboea, in honor of its deceased king Amphidamas. It was a contest after which only the name of the winner became well-known: Hesiod.

Homer may have written his great work, originating from the oral poetry which was previously all that existed, between 750 and 700 B.C. Judging by the prominence of the Ionian dialect in the poem, it seems it may have originated in Ionia, to the east of the Aegean, possibly on the island of Chios, located very close to Troy.

In the 500's B.C., a group of *rhapsodes* (professional reciters of epic poetry in ancient Greece), in Chios, known as the "Homeridae" (sons of Homer) claimed to exclusively recite his verses.

One of the Homeridae, Cynaethus of Chios, was known for reciting the *Hymn to Delian Apollo,* which he attributed to "a blind man who lived on the steep island of Chios."

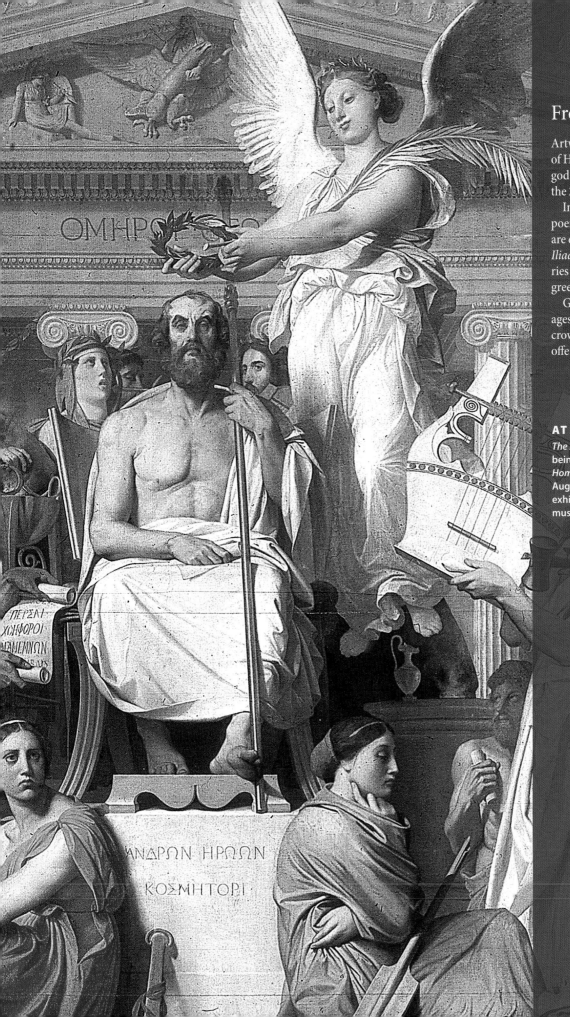

From Poet to God

Artwork showing the elevation of Homer from a human to a god are found from as early as the 200's B.C.

In the painting at left, the poems the *Iliad* and the *Odyssey* are embodied as women—the *Iliad* wears a red dress and carries a sword, the *Odyssey* is in a green dress and has an oar.

Great artists who, through the ages, were inspired by Homer, crowd around his throne and offer him gifts.

AT THE LOUVRE

The Apotheosis (raising of a human being to the rank of a god) *of Homer* (1827), the work of Jean Auguste Dominique Ingres, is exhibited at the famous Louvre museum in Paris.

Who Built It?

According to Homer, it was Odysseus's idea, but it was Epeius who is said to have built the famous Trojan horse out of pine from Mount Ida. Epeius, the son of Panopeus, is represented in the image to the left in a marble relief from 560 B.C. found on the Greek island of Samothrace and on view at the Louvre in Paris.

The Procession of the Trojan Horse into Troy, by Italian painter Giovanni Tiepolo (1696-1770).

Was There Really a Trojan Horse?

The Trojan Horse, mentioned in Book VIII of the *Odyssey*, is mostly considered to be a fantastic idea made up by Homer to dress up the less attractive idea of a simple siege machine.

The story of the Trojan horse was spoken of in Book VIII in a scene set at the Palace of Alcinous, King of the Phaeacians (a mythical Greek people), where Odysseus stayed. Odysseus addressed the blind bard, Demodocus, who livened up the events at the court, asking him to sing about the subject of the "wooden horse built by Epeius (EH peh uhs) with the help of Athena. Odysseus took this deceptive machine to the *acropolis* (city center) after filling it with soldiers who ruined Troy." Thus, it became known that the Achaeans went to sea after burning their own encampments, while Odysseus and his men were hidden inside a wooden horse that the Trojans brought through their walls and into their acropolis.

At first, the Trojans considered destroying the horse with swords or throwing it down from a high place, but they finally decided to leave it as an offering to the gods. This was their downfall, as "the most courageous Argives (Greeks from the city of Argos) who caused harm to the Teucers (Trojans) and brought about their death" came out of the horse.

THE HORSE IN THE AENEID

The Trojan horse also featured in the second book of the *Aeneid*, written in Latin in around 30 to 19 B.C. by the poet Virgil. In it, the character of the prophet Laocoon, who was opposed to bringing the horse into the acropolis, emerged with a well-known phrase: "I fear the Danaans (Greeks), even bringing gifts." The Trojan horse continued its triumphant journey in legend around the world. Neither Demodocus nor Aeneas, in either the *Odyssey* or the *Aeneid*, mentioned the number of men that were hidden inside. However, even some ancient authors doubted that the trick had occurred. For example, the opinion of Pausanius, a Greek geographer and historian from the A.D. 100's, was against the story of the Trojan horse having happened as told by Homer. Pausanius saw the real horse as likely to have been a siege engine, or machine, such as a battering ram, which the Achaeans used to knock down the walls of the highest part of the city.

It has also been interpreted as a metaphor for the new Greek fleet, since Homer called the ships "sea horses," seeing them as a symbol of Poseidon (god of the sea), who was said to have destroyed Troy with an earthquake.

The Trojan Horse

Homer mentions the horse in the *Odyssey,* as does Virgil in the *Aeneid.* But other sources tell the story of the Trojan horse, including Euripides (480-406 B.C.) in his play The *Trojan Women.*

SYMBOLISM
Horses were a frequent gift between kings of that time. To the Trojans, they stood for obedience to the gods.

Poseidon, a Possible Model

There are those who say that the Trojan horse could have been a reference to Poseidon, king of the depths of the ocean and land in Greek mythology.

An Empty Horse?

Barry Strauss, professor of History and Classics at Cornell University and author of the book *The Trojan War: A New History,* asserts that "the horse could have been used to infiltrate the city using elite troops, but the probability that they would have been discovered is very high. Although the traditional story of the Trojan horse cannot be ruled out, it seems more reasonable that it would have been empty, if it existed at all. There were simpler, less dangerous ways to *infiltrate* (sneak into) a city." Epic tradition offers few details about the Trojans' reaction, but it does discuss the sacking and later destruction of the city, in accordance with the laws of war at that time.

Troy Today

ILION

Aerial view of the hill where the remains of Troy were found. The creation of the first city, Troy I, is calculated at around 3000 B.C., while Troy IX, the last, is from the 300's A.D.

THE GOLDEN FLEECE
Jason, a mythical Greek hero, takes the Golden Fleece from the dragon that guards it. (The dragon has taken the form of a snake for the battle.) The woman in the sculpture is Medea, who used her magical powers to help Jason on his quest for the Golden Fleece.

Did the Trojan War Cause the Collapse of the Hittite Empire?

The German archaeologist Manfred Korfmann (1942-2005) came to this conclusion after a series of studies related to the origins of the name Wilusa, which was apparently the name used by the Hittites instead of Troy. In 1350 B.C., Wilusa became a tributary city of the Hittites, who suffered serious economic consequences as a result of the war, which was the beginning of their decline as a culture.

What Was the Connection Between the Golden Fleece and Troy?

According to some versions, the legend of the Golden Fleece was part of a military campaign by the Achaeans for the purpose of sailing to the Mycenaean kingdoms in an armed expedition against Troy. This legend, very popular in Homer's time, tells of Jason's journey with the Argonauts (named for their ship, the *Argo*) in search of the hide of a winged ram, known as the "Golden Fleece." It was found in the legendary country of Colchis, in the custody of a terrible dragon. Possession of the ram would give Jason a kingdom in Thessaly (a region of north-central Greece). During the journey, Jason and the Argonauts undertake a battle against Troy, defeating it and sacking the city. It is said that the only survivor was Priam. It was then that the Achaeans made the ram into a symbol of the great riches on the other side of the Aegean. However, access was fiercely controlled by the new Trojans, at the command of the survivor Priam, who imposed a toll and even blocked the strait. Consequently, only one option remained: the destruction of Troy.

HITTITES
Sculpture found in the palace at Tell Halaf, in Syria. The Hittites were a highly developed civilization. The Trojan War is thought to have been the beginning of the culture's decline.

Other Ideas on Troy

Some ideas about Troy are not commonly held, yet respected scholars have considered these ideas and opinions to be possible or even likely.

Was the *Iliad* Written by a Woman?

One idea that has circulated among scholars of ancient Greece raises a historical enigma. It states that it was not Homer who wrote the *Iliad* and the *Odyssey*, but someone else. Speculation about the true identity of this person runs wild. One such theory was raised by English author Samuel Butler (1835-1902), who maintained that these works were written by a woman. Butler dedicated many years of study to the subject and translated the *Iliad* and the *Odyssey* in prose; his translations continue to be very popular in the English-speaking world.

In 1897, Butler wrote a work titled *The Authoress of the Odyssey*, in which he suggested the possibility that the work had been written by a Sicilian princess, who appears in the story as Nausicaa (naw SIHK ay uh), one of the characters Odysseus encounters after leaving the island of the sea nymph Calypso and becoming shipwrecked yet again. Nausicaa was the daughter of King Alcinous and heard the story of his unexpected journey from Odysseus himself. Butler's writing makes it difficult to know whether or not he intended his idea seriously or was making fun of other research done on the subject at the time.

Another researcher, Richmond Lattimore (1906-1984), author of one of the most important English translations of both epics, indicated something similar in his essay "Homer: Who Was She?"

Finally, in his popular novel *Homer's Daughter*, published in the 1950's, British writer Robert Graves took up Butler's hypothesis and placed a Sicilian princess as the author of the epic poem generally attributed to Homer.

HOMER'S IDENTITY
There have always been questions as to his actual existence. Some scholars think the poet who wrote the *Iliad* and the *Odyssey* was a woman.

Places to See and Visit

Troy

TURKEY

For years, it was thought that Troy was no more than a legend, but today it is one of the most visited archaeological sites in the world. The ancient city of Troy, in what is now Turkey, is composed of nine archaeological sites superimposed on one another. A wooden replica of the famous horse from Homeric tradition greets visitors. At the site, visitors can see the city walls, the temple, the theater and the foundations of many homes.

OTHER PLACES OF INTEREST

MYCENAE
GREECE

The archaeological site of Mycenae, located northeast of the Peloponnesian peninsula, is the greatest remnant of the Mycenaean civilization, which dominated Greece from 2000 to 1000 B.C. The walls of the Mycenaean *acropolis* (city center) were built in a style known as "Cyclopean" because the blocks of stone used were so large that later peoples believed that they were the work of *Cyclopes* (one-eyed giants).

TIRYNS
GREECE

A Mycenaean archaeological site located on the Peloponnesian peninsula. The site was a fortress on a hill that was occupied for more than 7,000 years. It reached its zenith between 1400 and 1200 B.C. The most notable elements at Tiryns were a palace, tunnels, and passageways, and two rings of Cyclopean walls, the reason Homer called it "the city of the great walls." In mythology, this is the city in which Hercules (Heracles, in Greek) was born.

PUSHKIN MUSEUM OF FINE ARTS
RUSSIA

For years it was said that the gold from Priam's Treasure had been melted down. In 1993, however, the Pushkin Museum in Moscow confirmed that these objects were there. They had arrived in 1945 as spoils of war. Priam's Treasure had disappeared from Greece during World War II (1939-1945). The Soviet Army found the treasure in Berlin and moved it from the German capital to Moscow.

Glossary

Achaeans—Ancient people who lived on Greece's southern peninsula and on the islands of Crete, Rhodes, Cephalonia, and Ithaca.

Acropolis—Center of an ancient city.

Archaeologist—A scientist who studies past human cultures.

Archaic Period—The time period of approximately 800 B.C. to 400 B.C. in ancient Greece.

Civilization—A society or culture that has complex social, political, and economic institutions.

Cuneiform—The wedge-shaped characters used in the writing of ancient Babylonia, Assyria, Persia, and some other areas of the Near East.

Decipher—To convert a text from one language into another language or languages.

Epic—A long narrative poem, usually about the heroic deeds of divine beings and people in war or travel.

Hieroglyph—A picture, character, or symbol standing for a word, idea, or sound.

Hexameter—A line of poetry consisting of six feet or measures.

Mycenaean—Of or having to do with Mycenae, a very ancient city in southern Greece, or the civilization, culture, or art that flourished there from about 1500 B.C. to about 1100 B.C.

Prophesy—To foretell the future.

Siege—Surrounding a city or fortified place, cutting off all movement into and out from it, and usually attacking it.

Tell—A mound made up of the layers covering the ruins of an ancient city.

Glossary of Names

Achilles—The greatest of the Greek warriors. The son of Peleus, the king of Phthia in Thessaly, and Thetis, an immortal sea nymph. Soon after Achilles was born, Thetis dipped him in the River Styx, whose water would make him invulnerable, like a god. However, the immortalizing water did not touch the heel by which Thetis held him. During the Trojan War, Paris shot an arrow into Achilles's heel, and Achilles died from the wound.

Aeneas—A Trojan hero in Greek and Roman mythology. The son of the Trojan prince Anchises and the Greek goddess Aphrodite. When Troy fell, Aeneas fled with his father and his son, Ascanius, from the burning city. Eventually, Aeneas was said to have founded Rome.

Agamemnon—Leader of the Greek army that conquered in the Trojan War. Agamemnon was the king of Mycenae.

Aphrodite—The Greek goddess of love and beauty. In the works of Homer, Aphrodite was the daughter of the goddess Dione and Zeus, the king of the gods. In earlier myths, Aphrodite rose full-grown from sea foam. In the Trojan War, Aphrodite sided with Troy.

Apollo—The Greek god of the sun and also of poetry, music, and prophecy. Apollo was the son of Zeus, the king of the gods, and the goddess Leto. The goddess Artemis was Apollo's twin. In the Trojan War, Apollo sided with Troy.

Athena—The Greek goddess of warfare, wisdom, and arts and crafts. Athena was born full-grown, dressed in armor, from the head of Zeus. In the Trojan War, Athena sided with Greece.

Cassandra—The daughter of Priam and Hecuba, king and queen of Troy.

According to Homer, her beauty was so great that Apollo fell in love with her and gave her the gift of prophecy. But she did not return his love, and Apollo angrily punished her by ordering that no one should ever believe her prophecies. After the fall of Troy, Agamemnon took Cassandra as a slave to Mycenae, where she was murdered.

Eris—The goddess of strife and discord, a daughter of Zeus and Hera. Eris was not invited to a wedding, but she came as an uninvited guest. The seeds of the Trojan War are found in the argument Eris began between Aphrodite, Athena, and Hera at this wedding. In the Trojan War, Eris sided with Troy.

Hector—The greatest hero of the ancient city of Troy and the son of Priam, the king of Troy, and Hecuba. Hector is killed in battle by the Greek warrior Achilles.

Helen (of Troy)—The most beautiful woman in the world at the time of the Trojan War. Helen was the daughter of Zeus and Leda, a human being. According to one myth, Zeus appeared in the form of a swan when he visited Leda. Helen later hatched from a swan's egg. Helen was married to Menelaus, king of Sparta, and her abduction by the Trojan prince, Paris, is said to have been the cause of the Trojan War.

Hephaestus—The blacksmith of the gods in Greek mythology. The Greeks associated Hephaestus with volcanic areas. According to some myths, Hephaestus was married to Aphrodite. In the Trojan War, Hephaestus sided with Greece.

Hera—A goddess of life in Greek mythology. She was especially a protector of marriage and childbirth. Hera was the sister and wife of Zeus. In the Trojan War, Hera sided with Greece.

Laocoon—A Trojan priest, warned his people against the Greeks at Troy. When the Greek's left the Trojan Horse outside the walls of Troy, Laocoon cautioned them to destroy the horse, saying, "I fear the Greeks, even when bringing gifts."

Nausicaa—A maiden, daughter of the king of Phaeacia, who aids Odysseus on his travels after the Trojan War. She has no part in the war itself.

Odysseus—King of Ithaca and a brave and cunning Greek hero during the Trojan War.

Paris—Son of Priam, the king of Troy, and Hecuba. Paris's theft of Helen from her Greek husband leads up to the Trojan War, by some accounts.

Patroclus—Great friend of the warrior Achilles. When Achilles refused to continue fighting in the war, Patroclus wore Achilles's armor and was killed on the battlefield by Hector. In the Trojan War, Patroclus fought for Greece.

Peleus—A king of the Myrmidons and the father of Achilles.

Poseidon—The Greek god of the sea, earthquakes, and horses. In the Trojan War, Poseidon sided with Greece.

Priam—The last king of Troy and ruler of the city during the Trojan War with Greece.

Thetis—One of the Nereids—beautiful sea nymphs who attended the sea gods Poseidon and Amphitrite. Thetis was the mother of Achilles.

Zeus—The ruler of the gods in Greek mythology; a sky and weather god, especially associated with rain, thunder, and lightning.

For Further Information

Books

Crompton, Samuel Etinde. *Troy*. New York: Chelsea House, 2012. Print.

McCarty, Nick. *Troy: The Myth and Reality behind the Epic Legend*. New York: Rosen Pub., 2008. Print.

Olmstead, Kathleen, adapt. *The Iliad*. By Homer. Illus. Eric Freeberg. New York: Sterling, 2014. Print.

Rubalcaba, Jill, Eric H. Cline, and Sarah S. Brannen. *Digging for Troy: From Homer to Hisarlik*. Watertown, MA: Charlesbridge, 2011. Print.

Zamorsky, Tania, adapt. *The Odyssey*. By Homer. Illus. Eric Freeberg. New York: Sterling, 2011. Print.

Websites

"Archaeological Site of Troy." *UNESCO World Heritage Centre*. UNESCO, 2014. Web. 24 Feb. 2014.

"In Our Time: The Trojan War." *BBC Radio 4*. BBC, 31 May 2012. Web. 24 Feb. 2014.

Korfmann, Manfred. "Was There a Trojan War?" *Archaeology*. Archaeological Institute of America, May-June 2004. Web. 24 Feb. 2014.

Lovgren, Stefan. "Is Troy True? The Evidence Behind Movie Myth." *National Geographic*. National Geographic Society, 14 May 2004. Web. 24 Feb. 2014.

"The Trojan War." *British Museum*. Trustees of the British Museum, n.d. Web. 24 Feb. 2014.

Index